Sports Illustrated Kids: Legend vs. Legend

STEVE AUSTIN

VS.

DWAYNE JOHNSON

WRESTLING LEGENDS FACE OFF

by Elliott Smith

CAPSTONE PRESS
a capstone imprint

Published by Capstone Press, an imprint of Capstone
1710 Roe Crest Drive, North Mankato, Minnesota 56003
capstonepub.com

Copyright © 2025 by Capstone. All rights reserved. No part of this publication may be reproduced in whole or in part, or stored in a retrieval system, or transmitted in any form or by any means, electronic, mechanical, photocopying, recording, or otherwise, without written permission of the publisher.

SPORTS ILLUSTRATED KIDS is a trademark of ABG-SI LLC. Used with permission.

Library of Congress Cataloging-in-Publication Data is available on
the Library of Congress website.

ISBN: 9781669089421 (hardcover)
ISBN: 9781669089551 (paperback)
ISBN: 9781669089469 (ebook PDF)

Summary: Steve Austin and Dwayne Johnson are wrestling superstars! Between the two, Austin has an amazing finishing move, but Johnson has more WWE titles. So which one is the all-time best? Decide for yourself by comparing the fantastic feats and stunning stats of two legendary pro wrestlers!

Editorial Credits
Editor: Ericka Smith; Designer: Tracy Davies; Media Researcher: Svetlana Zhurkin; Production Specialist: Whitney Schaefer

Image Credits
Alamy: CelebrityArchaeology/PhotoLink/John Barett, 17, Cinematic, 24, Gavin Rodgers, 14, kolvenbach, 8, 12, MediaPunch Inc/PhotoLink/John Barrett, 21, 27, PhotoLink/John Barrett, 22, Zuma Press/Globe Photos, 26; Associated Press: File/Mel Evans, 18, WWE Corp./Paul Abell, 11, WWE/Jonathan Bachman, 5; Getty Images: FilmMagic/George Napolitano, 7, Hulton Archive, cover (left), 28, Icon Sportswire/Pximages/Louis Grasse, cover (right), Sports Imagery/Ron Elkman, 13, Tim Nwachukwu, 4, 10, WireImage/Eugene Gologursky, 20, WireImage/George Pimentel, 9, 19, WireImage/Kevin Mazur, 6, 29, WireImage/Theo Wargo, 16; Newscom: PhotoLink/John Barrett, 15, Splash News/Jackie Brown, 23; Shutterstock: Dfree, 25, saicle (background), cover and throughout

Any additional websites and resources referenced in this book are not maintained, authorized, or sponsored by Capstone. All product and company names are trademarks™ or registered® trademarks of their respective holders.

Printed and bound in China. PO 6098

CONTENTS

Wrestling Warriors Square Off! 4
Height and Weight 6
Matches Wrestled 8
Finishing Moves 10
Top Feuds 12
Victories 14
Tag Team Partners 16
WrestleMania Wins 18
Titles Won 20
Catchphrases 22
Entertainment 24
Head-to-Head 26
Who Is the Best? 28

    Glossary 30
    Read More 31
    Internet Sites 31
    Index 32
    About the Author 32

*** *All stats current through the 2023 season.* ***
Words in **bold** appear in the glossary.

Wrestling Warriors Square Off!

Dwayne "the Rock" Johnson and "Stone Cold" Steve Austin are two of the greatest wrestlers of all time. They're World Wrestling Entertainment (WWE) superstars. Johnson is known for his strength. Austin relies on skill.

But which wrestler is the best? Let's find out!

Dwayne Johnson

Steve Austin

THE MATCHUP	Born	City
Johnson	May 2, 1972	Hayward, California
Austin	Dec. 18, 1964	Victoria, Texas

Height and Weight

The best wrestlers are usually larger than life. Imagine standing in the ring as the Rock flexes his 20-inch **biceps**! Or watching Stone Cold's huge frame fly off the top rope! For these two heavyweights, size matters!

Johnson at WrestleMania in 2012

Austin at a World Wresting Entertainment Hall of Fame event in 2011

THE MATCHUP	Height	Weight (approximate)
Johnson	6 feet, 4 inches (193 centimeters)	260 pounds (118 kilograms)
Austin	6 feet, 2 inches (188 cm)	252 pounds (114 kg)

Matches Wrestled

Staying in the ring is key to a wrestler's success. Some top wrestlers perform more than 300 days a year! Austin has had almost 1,500 **matches**. Johnson's been in the ring more than 850 times. That's a lot of body slams and flying leaps.

Austin in a match against the Undertaker in 2002

Johnson competing against Hulk Hogan during WrestleMania in 2002

THE MATCHUP	Matches
Austin	1,479
Johnson	855

Finishing Moves

The Rock's and Stone Cold's finishing moves are top-notch. The People's Elbow, an elbow drop, and Rock Bottom, a body slam, are the Rock's specialties. The Stone Cold Stunner is a quick, powerful shoulder hit to the head. It's one of the most recognizable moves in wrestling!

Johnson using his Rock Bottom move on John Cena

Austin using the Stone Cold Stunner on Booker T

THE MATCHUP	Finishing Moves
Johnson	People's Elbow, Rock Bottom
Austin	Stone Cold Stunner

Top Feuds

Stone Cold and the Rock had a years-long **feud** with each other. But they had other **epic** battles too. Stone Cold squared off against his **rival** Triple H for several **championship** titles. The Rock and fellow superstar John Cena clashed multiple times.

Stone Cold facing off against the Undertaker in 2002

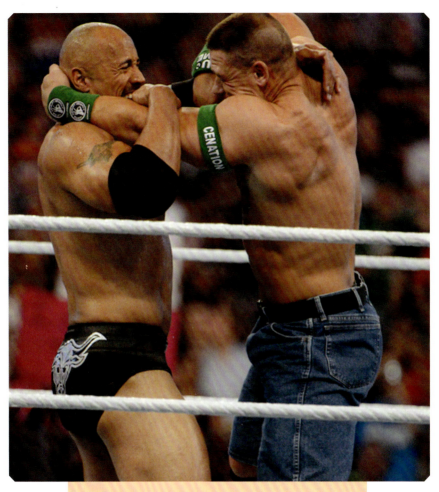

The Rock wrestling with Cena in 2012

THE MATCHUP	Biggest Rivals
Austin	Bret Hart, Triple H, the Undertaker
Johnson	John Cena, Kurt Angle, Mankind

Victories

Both wrestlers have many victories. The Rock has 452 career wins. In 2000 alone, he won 97 matches! Stone Cold has 816 victories. His best year was 1998. He won 124 matches that year!

Johnson in a 2000 match against Triple H

Austin celebrating a win in 1998

THE MATCHUP	Wins
Johnson	452
Austin	816

Tag Team Partners

Joining forces with others can help wrestlers succeed in the ring. But finding the *right* partner is key. Austin's most successful pairing was with his rival Triple H. Johnson started wrestling as part of a group. He often paired up with Kane.

Stone Cold with Triple H

The Rock and Kane in 1998

THE MATCHUP	Tag Partners
Austin	Dude Love, Kurt Angle, Shawn Michaels, Triple H
Johnson	Chris Jericho, D'Lo Brown, Kane, Mankind

WrestleMania Wins

WrestleMania is the most important WWE event. Only the best get to go toe-to-toe in the Super Bowl of wrestling. The Rock and Stone Cold both shined on the big stage. The Rock had six wins in 11 matches. Stone Cold had eight matches and six wins.

The Rock competing against Cena in the 2013 WrestleMania event

Stone Cold in a match against Razor Ramon during WrestleMania in 2002

THE MATCHUP	WrestleMania Matches	WrestleMania Wins
Johnson	11	6
Austin	8	6

Titles Won

All wrestlers want to win a championship. And there are several titles wrestlers can win. Johnson has 17 titles. He won the WWE Championship title an amazing eight times! Stone Cold won 12 titles. Four of those wins were tag team titles.

Johnson with one of his championship belts during a 2013 WrestleMania press conference

Austin in the ring with a championship belt in 2001

THE MATCHUP	WWE Intercontinental Championship Titles	World Heavyweight Championship Titles	World Tag Team Championship Titles	WWE Championship Titles
Johnson	2	2	5	8
Austin	2	0	4	6

Catchphrases

Capturing the crowd is a key part of wrestling. Austin and Johnson are the best to ever grab a microphone. For Stone Cold, a simple "WHAT?" was enough to get fans cheering. But the Rock's **slogans** are one of a kind. Fans chanted "Can you smell what the Rock is cookin'?" from **arenas** coast to coast.

Stone Cold wearing a T-shirt with one of his catchphrases

The Rock wearing gear with one of his catchphrases during WrestleMania in 2014

THE MATCHUP	Top Catchphrases
Austin	"WHAT?" "Austin 3:16" "Cuz Stone Cold said so!"
Johnson	"Can you smell what the Rock is cookin'?" "Finally!" "It doesn't matter!" "Know your role." "Just bring it."

Entertainment

Both Johnson and Austin had talent outside the ring. Austin starred in 14 movies and a few TV shows. He even hosted a reality TV show. Johnson's breakout **role** was in *The Mummy Returns*. Then, he starred in a series of blockbuster action and superhero films. He's been in 48 movies so far.

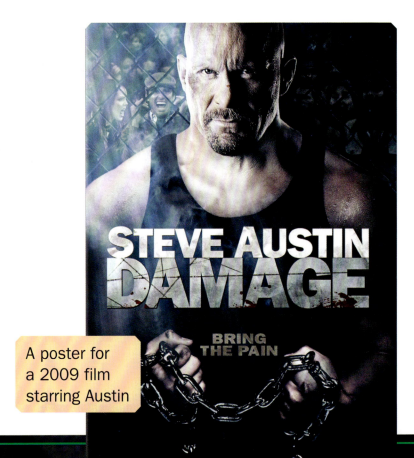

A poster for a 2009 film starring Austin

Johnson at the premiere for the 2019 movie *Jumanji: The Next Level*

THE MATCHUP	Movies
Austin	14
Johnson	48

Head-to-Head

Austin and Johnson had some of their best matches against each other. They faced off seven times. They first met in 1997 for the Intercontinental title. But their three matches at WrestleMania are legendary. Austin won two of them.

Austin and Johnson competing during WrestleMania in 2001

Johnson and Austin during a 1999 match

THE MATCHUP	Head-to-Head Wins
Austin	6
Johnson	1

Who Is the Best?

Dwayne "the Rock" Johnson and "Stone Cold" Steve Austin are amazing wrestlers. Johnson won more titles. But Austin wins the head-to-head matchup. Stone Cold has the better finishing move. But the Rock's mic skills are unbeatable. Both helped make wrestling popular.

Who is the best wrestler? You make the call!

Austin in 2000

Johnson at WrestleMania in 2012

Glossary

arena (uh-REE-nuh)—a large area that is used for sports or entertainment

biceps (BY-seps)—the muscle on the front of a person's arm responsible for bending the arm at the elbow

championship (CHAM-pee-uhn-ship)—a final match that determines who will be the overall winner

epic (EP-ik)—very big or impressive

feud (FYOOD)—a long-lasting disagreement between people

match (MACH)—a game or competition

rival (RYE-vuhl)—someone with whom you compete

role (ROHL)—an actor's part in a movie, TV series, or play

slogan (SLOH-guhn)—a phrase or motto used by a business, a group, or an individual

Read More

Green, Rob. *The Rock: Learn All About Your Favorite Wrestling Star*. Self-published, 2023.

Leed, Percy. *Pro Wrestling Superstars*. Minneapolis: Lerner, 2024.

Schuh, Mari. *What You Never Knew About Dwayne Johnson*. North Mankato, MN: Capstone, 2023.

Internet Sites

Britannica Kids: Wrestling
kids.britannica.com/kids/article/wrestling/353938

Kiddle: History of WWE Facts for Kids
kids.kiddle.co/History_of_WWE

Sports Illustrated Kids: Wrestling
sikids.com/tag/wrestling

Index

Angle, Kurt, 13, 17

birthdays, 5
birthplaces, 5
Booker T, 11

career wins, 14–15
catchphrases, 22–23, 28
Cena, John, 10, 12, 13, 18

D'Lo Brown, 17
Dude Love, 17

entertainment, 24–25

finishing moves, 10–11, 28

Hart, Bret, 13
head-to-head matches, 26–27, 28
height, 7

Hulk Hogan, 9

Jericho, Chris, 17

Kane, 16, 17

Mankind, 13, 17
matches, 8–9
Michaels, Shawn, 17

Razor Ramon, 19

titles, 12, 20–21, 26, 28
Triple H, 12, 13, 14, 16, 17

Undertaker, 8, 12, 13

weight, 7
WrestleMania, 6, 9, 18–19, 20, 23, 26, 29
WWE Hall of Fame, 7

About the Author

Elliott Smith is a freelance writer, editor, and author. He has covered a wide variety of subjects—including sports, entertainment, and travel—for newspapers, magazines, and websites. He has written more than 70 children's books, both fiction and nonfiction. He lives in the Washington, DC, area with his wife and two children.